AF201093

Impressum
Verlag: BABADADA GmbH, Nedderfeld 112 , 22529 Hamburg
Geschäftsführer / Verlagsleitung: Harald Hof
Druck: Books on Demand GmbH, In de Tarpen 42, 22848 Norderstedt

Imprint
Publisher: BABADADA GmbH, Nedderfeld 112 , 22529 Hamburg, Germany
Managing Director / Publishing direction: Harald Hof
Print: Books on Demand GmbH, In de Tarpen 42, 22848 Norderstedt

divide
divide

186/2

board
board

classroom
classroom

school yard
school yard

teacher
teacher

paper
paper

write
write

pen
pen

desk
desk

ruler
ruler

book
book

pupil
pupil

satchel

satchel

pencil case

pencil case

pencil

pencil

pencil sharpener

pencil sharpener

rubber

rubber

drawing pad

drawing pad

drawing

drawing

paintbrush

paintbrush

paint box

paint box

scissors

scissors

glue

glue

exercise book

exercise book

homework

homework

number

number

add

add

subtract

subtract

multiply

multiply

calculate

calculate

letter

letter

ABCDEFG
HIJKLMN
OPQRSTU
VWXYZ

alphabet

alphabet

word

word

text
text

read
read

chalk
chalk

lesson
lesson

register
register

examination
exam

certificate
certificate

school uniform
school uniform

education
education

encyclopedia
encyclopedia

university
university

microscope
microscope

map
map

waste-paper basket
paper bin

hotel
hotel

hostel
hostel

currency exchange office
bureau de change

suitcase
suitcase

car
car

language

language

yes / no

yes / no

Okay

Okay

hello

hello

translator

translator

Thank you

Thank you

how much is...?

how much does ... cost?

I don't get it

I do not understand

problem

problem

Good evening!

Good evening!

Good morning!

Good morning!

Good night!

Good night!

goodbye

bye bye

direction

direction

luggage

luggage

bag

bag

backpack

backpack

guest

guest

room

room

sleeping bag

sleeping bag

tent

tent

tourist information

tourist information

beach

beach

credit card

credit card

breakfast

breakfast

lunch

lunch

dinner

dinner

Ticket

ticket

elevator

lift

stamp

stamp

border

border

customs

customs

embassy

embassy

visa

visa

passport

passport

airplane
aeroplane

ship
ship

fire truck
fire engine

bus
bus

truck
truck

motorboat
motorboat

bike
bike

car
car

ferry
ferry

boat
boat

motorbike
motorbike

police car
police car

racing car
racing car

rental car
rental car

car sharing
car sharing

tow truck
breakdown truck

garbage truck
refuse truck

engine
motor

fuel
fuel

fuel station
petrol station

traffic sign
traffic sign

traffic
traffic

traffic jam
traffic jam

parking lot
car park

train station
train station

tracks
tracks

train
train

tram
tram

wagon
carriage

helicopter

helicopter

airport

airport

tower

tower

passenger

passenger

container

container

carton

carton

cart

cart

basket

basket

take off / land

take off / land

## city

## city

village

village

city center

city centre

house

house

## City scene labels

- movie theater / cinema
- advert / advert
- street light / street light
- street / street
- taxi / taxi
- snack shop / snack shop
- pedestrian / pedestrian
- sidewalk / pavement
- zebra crossing / zebra crossing
- dumpster / bin
- crossing / crossing
- traffic lights / traffic lights

CINEMA

hut
hut

apartment
flat

train station
train station

city hall
town hall

museum
museum

school
school

university

university

bank

bank

hospital

hospital

hotel

hotel

pharmacy

pharmacy

office

office

book shop

book shop

shop

shop

flower shop

florist's

supermarket

supermarket

market

market

department store

department store

fishmonger's shop

fishmonger's

mall

shopping centre

harbor

harbour

park
park

bench
bench

bridge
bridge

stairs
stairs

subway
underground

tunnel
tunnel

bus stop
bus stop

bar
bar

restaurant
restaurant

postbox
postbox

street sign
road sign

parking meter
parking meter

zoo
zoo

swimming pool
swimming pool

mosque
mosque

city - city

13

farm
farm

pollution
pollution

cemetery
graveyard

church
church

playground
playground

temple
temple

## landscape
## landscape

leaf
leaf

signpost
signpost

path
way

meadow
meadow

stone
stone

hiker
hiker

tree
tree

river
river

grass
grass

flower
flower

valley

valley

hill

hill

lake

lake

forest

forest

desert

desert

volcano

volcano

castle

castle

rainbow

rainbow

mushroom

mushroom

palm tree

palm tree

mosquito

mosquito

fly

fly

ant

ant

bee

bee

spider

spider

beetle

beetle

frog

frog

squirrel

squirrel

hedgehog

hedgehog

hare

hare

owl

owl

bird

bird

swan

swan

boar

boar

deer

deer

moose

moose

dam

dam

wind turbine

wind turbine

solar panel

solar panel

climate

climate

waiter
waiter

menu
menu

chair
chair

soup
soup

pizza
pizza

cutlery
cutlery

tablecloth
tablecloth

starter
starter

main course
main course

dessert
dessert

drinks
drinks

food
food

bottle
bottle

fast food

fast food

street food

street food

teapot

teapot

sugar bowl

sugar bowl

portion

portion

espresso machine

espresso machine

high chair

high chair

bill

bill

tray

tray

knife

knife

fork

fork

spoon

spoon

teaspoon

teaspoon

serviette

serviette

glass

glass

plate
plate

soup plate
soup plate

saucer
saucer

sauce
sauce

salt shaker
salt cellar

pepper mill
pepper mill

vinegar
vinegar

oil
oil

spices
spices

ketchup
ketchup

mustard
mustard

mayonnaise
mayonnaise

special offer
special offer

FOR

customer
customer

dairy products
dairy

fruit
fruit

shopping cart
trolley

butcher's shop
butcher's

bakery
baker's

weigh
weigh

vegetables
vegetables

meat
meat

frozen food
frozen food

cold cuts
...............
cold meat

canned food
...............
tinned food

detergent
...............
washing powder

candy
...............
sweets

household products
...............
household products

cleaning products
...............
cleaning products

sales representative
...............
salesperson

cash register
...............
till

cashier
...............
cashier

shopping list
...............
shopping list

opening hours
...............
opening hours

wallet
...............
wallet

credit card
...............
credit card

bag
...............
bag

plastic bag
...............
plastic bag

## drinks

water

water

juice

juice

milk

milk

coke

coke

wine

wine

beer

beer

alcohol

alcohol

cocoa

cocoa

tea

tea

coffee

coffee

espresso

espresso

cappuccino

cappuccino

banana

banana

apple

apple

orange

orange

melon

melon

lemon

lemon

carrot

carrot

garlic

garlic

bamboo

bamboo

onion

onion

mushroom

mushroom

nuts

nuts

noodles

noodles

spaghetti

spaghetti

rice

rice

salad

salad

fries

chips

fried potatoes

fried potatoes

pizza

pizza

hamburger

hamburger

sandwich

sandwich

escalope

cutlet

ham

ham

salami

salami

sausage

sausage

chicken

chicken

roast

roast

fish

fish

porridge oats

porridge oats

muesli

muesli

cornflakes

cornflakes

flour

flour

croissant

croissant

bread roll

bread roll

bread

bread

toast

toast

cookies

biscuits

butter

butter

curd

curd

cake

cake

egg

egg

fried egg

fried egg

cheese

cheese

ice cream

ice cream

sugar

sugar

honey

honey

jelly

jam

nougat cream

chocolate spread

curry

curry

food - food

farm house
farmhouse

straw bale
straw bale

barn
barn

field
field

horse
horse

trailer
trailer

foal
foal

tractor
tractor

donkey
donkey

lamb
lamb

sheep
sheep

goat
goat

cow
cow

calf
calf

pig
pig

piglet
piglet

bull
bull

goose

goose

duck

duck

chick

chick

hen

hen

cockerel

cock

rat

rat

cat

cat

mouse

mouse

ox

ox

dog

dog

dog house

doghouse

garden hose

garden hose

watering can

watering can

scythe

scythe

plow

plough

farm - farm

sickle

sickle

hoe

hoe

pitchfork

pitchfork

axe

axe

pushcart

wheelbarrow

trough

trough

milk can

milk can

sack

sack

fence

fence

stable

stable

greenhouse

greenhouse

soil

soil

seed

seed

fertilizer

fertilizer

combine harvester

combine harvester

harvest

harvest

harvest

harvest

yams

yams

wheat

wheat

soya

soy

potato

potato

corn

corn

rapeseed

rapeseed

fruit tree

fruit tree

manioc

cassava

grain

cereals

chimney
chimney

roof
roof

downspout
drain pipe

window
window

garage
garage

doorbell
doorbell

door
door

trash can
rubbish bin

mailbox
letterbox

garden
garden

living room
living room

bathroom
bathroom

kitchen
kitchen

bedroom
bedroom

kids room
child's room

dining room
dining room

floor

floor

wall

wall

ceiling

ceiling

cellar

cellar

sauna

sauna

balcony

balcony

terrace

terrace

pool

pool

lawn mower

lawn mower

sheet

sheet

bedspread

bedspread

bed

bed

broom

broom

bucket

bucket

switch

switch

wallpaper
wallpaper

picture
picture

lamp
lamp

shelf
shelf

cabinet
cupboard

television
television

fireplace
fireplace

flower
flower

cushion
cushion

vase
vase

sofa
sofa

remote control
remote control

carpet
carpet

drape
curtain

table
table

chair
chair

rocking chair
rocking chair

armchair
armchair

book
book

blanket
blanket

decoration
decoration

firewood
firewood

film
film

stereo system
hi-fi equipment

key
key

newspaper
newspaper

painting
painting

poster
poster

radio
radio

notebook
notepad

vacuum cleaner
hoover

cactus
cactus

candle
candle

fridge
fridge

microwave oven
microwave oven

kitchen scales
kitchen scales

toaster
toaster

laundry detergent
detergent

freezer
freezer

stove
oven

trash can
rubbish bin

dishwasher
dishwasher

cooker
cooker

pot
pot

cast-iron pot
cast-iron pot

wok / kadai
wok / kadai

pan
pan

kettle
kettle

steamer

steamer

baking tray

baking tray

crockery

crockery

mug

mug

bowl

bowl

chopsticks

chopsticks

ladle

ladle

spatula

spatula

whisk

whisk

strainer

strainer

sieve

sieve

grater

grater

mortar

mortar

barbecue

barbecue

fireplace

open fire

chopping board

chopping board

rolling pin

rolling pin

corkscrew

corkscrew

can

can

can opener

can opener

oven cloth

pot holder

sink

sink

brush

brush

sponge

sponge

blender

blender

deep freezer

deep freezer

baby bottle

baby bottle

tap

tap

heating
heating

shower
shower

towel
towel

shower curtain
shower curtain

bubble bath
bubble bath

bathtub
bathtub

glass
glass

washing machine
washing machine

tap
tap

tiles
tiles

potty
potty

sink
sink

| | | |
|---|---|---|
| toilet<br>toilet | squat toilet<br>squat toilet | bidet<br>bidet |
| urinal<br>urinal | toilet paper<br>toilet paper | toilet brush<br>toilet brush |

toothbrush

toothbrush

toothpaste

toothpaste

dental floss

dental floss

wash

wash

hand shower

handheld shower

douche

douche

basin

basin

back brush

back brush

soap

soap

shower gel

shower gel

shampoo

shampoo

flannel

flannel

drain

drain

creme

cream

deodorant

deodorant

mirror

mirror

hand mirror

hand mirror

razor

razor

shaving foam

shaving foam

aftershave

aftershave

comb

comb

brush

brush

hair-dryer

hair dryer

hairspray

hairspray

makeup

makeup

lipstick

lipstick

nail varnish

nail varnish

cotton wool

cotton wool

nail scissors

nail scissors

perfume

perfume

bathroom - bathroom

washbag

washbag

stool

stool

weighing scales

weighing scale

bathrobe

bathrobe

rubber gloves

rubber gloves

tampon

tampon

sanitary towel

sanitary towel

chemical toilet

chemical toilet

# kids room
## child's room

alarm clock
alarm clock

cuddly toy
cuddly toy

toy car
toy car

rattle
rattle

doll's house
doll's house

present
present

balloon
balloon

bed
bed

stroller
pram

deck of cards
deck of cards

jigsaw
jigsaw

comic
comic

lego bricks
lego bricks

toy blocks
building blocks

action figure
action figure

romper suit
romper suit

frisbee
Frisbee

mobile
mobile

board game
board game

dice
dice

model train set
model train set

pacifier
dummy

party
party

picture book
picture book

ball
ball

doll
doll

play
play

sandpit

sandpit

swing

swing

toys

toys

video game console

video game console

tricycle

tricycle

teddy bear

teddy bear

wardrobe

wardrobe

# clothing

## clothing

socks

socks

stockings

stockings

tights

tights

scarf
scarf

belt
belt

umbrella
umbrella

t-shirt
t-shirt

boots
boots

slippers
slippers

sneakers
trainers

sandals
sandals

shoes
shoes

rubber boots
rubber boots

underwear
underpants

bra
bra

undershirt
vest

body
body

pants
trousers

jeans
jeans

skirt
skirt

blouse
blouse

shirt
shirt

pullover
pullover

sweater
hoodie

blazer
blazer

jacket
jacket

coat
coat

raincoat
raincoat

costume
costume

dress
dress

wedding dress
wedding dress

suit

suit

nightgown

nightgown

pajamas

pyjamas

sari

sari

headscarf

headscarf

turban

turban

burka

burqa

kaftan

kaftan

abaya

abaya

swimsuit

swimsuit

trunks

trunks

shorts

shorts

tracksuit

tracksuit

apron

apron

gloves

gloves

button
button

glasses
glasses

bracelet
bracelet

necklace
necklace

ring
ring

earring
earring

cap
cap

coat hanger
coat hanger

hat
hat

tie
tie

zip
zipper

helmet
helmet

braces
braces

school uniform
school uniform

uniform
uniform

bib
bib

pacifier
dummy

diaper
nappy

server
server

filing cabinet
filing cabinet

printer
printer

monitor
monitor

paper
paper

mouse
mouse

desk
desk

folder
folder

keyboard
keyboard

waste-paper basket
paper bin

chair
chair

computer
computer

coffee mug
coffee mug

calculator
calculator

internet
internet

laptop

laptop

letter

letter

message

message

cell phone

mobile

network

network

photocopier

photocopier

software

software

telephone

telephone

plug socket

plug socket

fax machine

fax machine

form

form

document

document

buy

buy

pay

pay

trade

trade

money

money

dollar

dollar

euro

euro

yen

yen

rouble

rouble

Swiss franc

Swiss franc

renminbi yuan

renminbi yuan

rupee

rupee

cash point

cashpoint

currency exchange office

bureau de change

gold

gold

silver

silver

oil

oil

energy

energy

price

price

contract

contract

tax

tax

stock

stock

work

work

employee

employee

employer

employer

factory

factory

shop

shop

economy - economy

police officer
police officer

fireman
fireman

pilot
pilot

doctor
doctor

cook
cook

gardener

gardener

carpenter

carpenter

seamstress

seamstress

judge

judge

chemist

chemist

actor

actor

bus driver

bus driver

taxi driver

taxi driver

fisherman

fisherman

cleaning lady

cleaning lady

roofer

roofer

waiter

waiter

hunter

hunter

painter

painter

baker

baker

electrician

electrician

builder

builder

engineer

engineer

butcher

butcher

plumber

plumber

postman

postman

soldier

soldier

architect

architect

cashier

cashier

florist

florist

hairdresser

hairdresser

conductor

conductor

mechanic

mechanic

captain

captain

dentist

dentist

scientist

scientist

rabbi

rabbi

imam

imam

monk

monk

pastor

clergyman

hammer
hammer

pliers
pliers

screwdriver
screwdriver

wrench
spanner

torch
torch

excavator
digger

toolbox
toolbox

ladder
ladder

saw
saw

nails
nails

drill
drill

repair

repair

shovel

shovel

Damn!

Damn!

dustpan

dustpan

paint can

paint pot

screws

screws

## musical instruments

## musical instruments

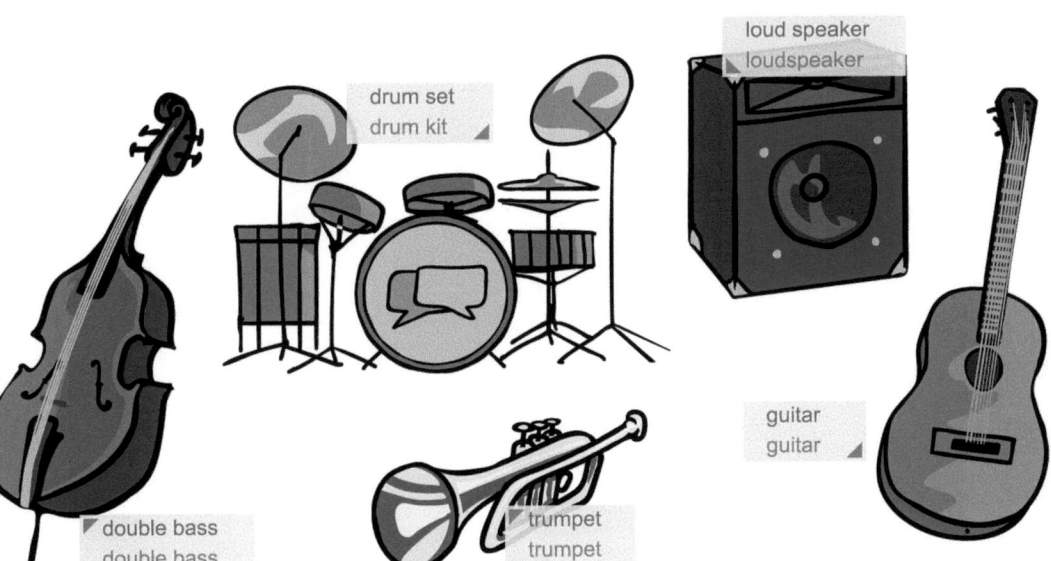

loud speaker
loudspeaker

drum set
drum kit

guitar
guitar

double bass
double bass

trumpet
trumpet

piano

piano

violin

violin

bass

bass

timpani

timpani

drums

drums

keyboard

keyboard

saxophone

saxophone

flute

flute

microphone

microphone

entrance
entrance

tiger
tiger

cage
cage

zebra
zebra

animal feed
animal feed

panda
panda

animals

animals

elephant

elephant

kangaroo

kangaroo

rhino

rhino

gorilla

gorilla

bear

bear

camel

camel

ostrich

ostrich

lion

lion

monkey

monkey

flamingo

flamingo

parrot

parrot

polar bear

polar bear

penguin

penguin

shark

shark

peacock

peacock

snake

snake

crocodile

crocodile

zookeeper

zookeeper

seal

seal

jaguar

jaguar

pony

pony

leopard

leopard

hippo

hippo

giraffe

giraffe

eagle

eagle

boar

boar

fish

fish

turtle

turtle

walrus

walrus

fox

fox

gazelle

gazelle

American football
American football

cycling
cycling

tennis
tennis

basketball
basketball

swimming
swimming

boxing
boxing

ice hockey
ice hockey

soccer
football

badminton
badminton

athletics
athletics

handball
handball

skiing
skiing

polo
polo

jump
jump

laugh
laugh

hug
hug

walk
walk

sing
sing

dream
dream

pray
pray

kiss
kiss

write

write

draw

draw

show

show

push

push

give

give

take

take

have
have

do
do

be
be

stand
stand

run
run

pull
pull

throw
throw

fall
fall

lie
lie

wait
wait

carry
carry

sit
sit

get dressed
get dressed

sleep
sleep

wake up
wake up

look at

look at

cry

cry

stroke

stroke

comb

comb

talk

talk

understand

understand

ask

ask

listen

listen

drink

drink

eat

eat

tidy up

tidy up

love

love

cook

cook

drive

drive

fly

fly

activities - activities

sail

sail

calculate

calculate

read

read

learn

learn

work

work

marry

marry

sew

sew

brush teeth

brush teeth

kill

kill

smoke

smoke

send

send

grandmother
grandmother

grandfather
grandfather

father
father

mother
mother

baby
baby

daughter
daughter

son
son

guest

guest

aunt

aunt

uncle

uncle

brother

brother

sister

sister

forehead
forehead

eye
eye

shoulder
shoulder

finger
finger

face
face

chin
chin

hand
hand

breast
breast

leg
leg

arm
arm

baby

baby

man

man

woman

woman

girl

girl

boy

boy

head

head

back
back

belly
belly

navel
belly button

toe
toe

heel
heel

bone
bone

hip
hip

knee
knee

elbow
elbow

nose
nose

buttocks
bottom

skin
skin

cheek
cheek

ear
ear

lip
lip

mouth

mouth

tooth

tooth

tongue

tongue

brain

brain

heart

heart

muscle

muscle

lung

lung

liver

liver

stomach

stomach

kidneys

kidneys

sex

sex

condom

condom

ovum

ovum

semen

semen

pregnancy

pregnancy

body - body

menstruation

menstruation

vagina

vagina

penis

penis

eyebrow

eyebrow

hair

hair

neck

neck

hospital
hospital

ambulance
ambulance

wheelchair
wheelchair

fracture
fracture

doctor
doctor

emergency room
emergency room

nurse
nurse

emergency
emergency

unconscious
unconscious

pain
pain

injury

injury

bleeding

bleeding

heart attack

heart attack

stroke

stroke

allergy

allergy

cough

cough

fever

fever

flu

flu

diarrhea

diarrhoea

headache

headache

cancer

cancer

diabetes

diabetes

surgeon

surgeon

scalpel

scalpel

operation

operation

CT

CT

x-ray

x-ray

ultrasound

ultrasound

face mask

face mask

disease

disease

waiting room

waiting room

crutch

crutch

plaster

plaster

bandage

bandage

injection

injection

stethoscope

stethoscope

stretcher

stretcher

clinical thermometer

clinical thermometer

birth

birth

overweight

overweight

hearing aid

hearing aid

disinfectant

disinfectant

infection

infection

virus

virus

HIV / AIDS

HIV / AIDS

medicine

medicine

vaccination

vaccination

tablets

tablets

pill

pill

emergency call

emergency call

blood pressure monitor

blood pressure monitor

ill / healthy

sick / healthy

Help!
Help!

alarm
alarm

assault
assault

attack
attack

danger
danger

emergency exit
emergency exit

Fire!
Fire!

fire extinguisher
fire extinguisher

accident
accident

first-aid kit
first-aid kit

SOS
SOS

police
police

Europe

Europe

North America

North America

South America

South America

Africa

Africa

Asia

Asia

Australia

Australia

Atlantic

Atlantic

Pacific

Pacific

Indian Ocean

Indian Ocean

Antarctic Ocean

Antarctic Ocean

Arctic Ocean

Arctic Ocean

North pole

North Pole

South pole

South Pole

Antarctica

Antarctica

earth

Earth

land

land

sea

sea

island

island

nation

nation

state

state

clock face

clock face

hour hand

hour hand

minute hand

minute hand

second hand

second hand

What time is it?

What time is it?

day

day

time

time

now

now

digital watch

digital watch

minute

minute

hour

hour

clock - clock

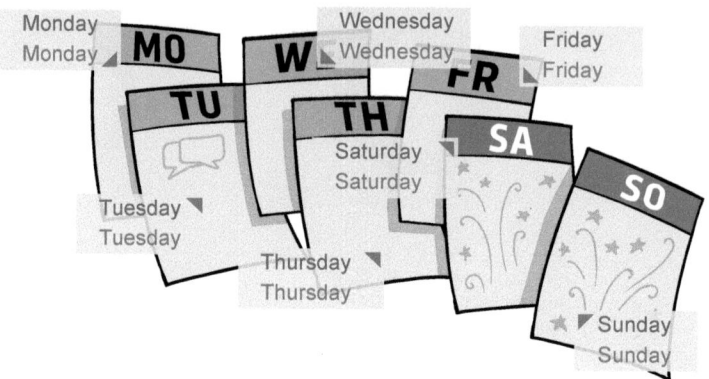

Monday
Monday

Wednesday
Wednesday

Friday
Friday

Tuesday
Tuesday

Saturday
Saturday

Thursday
Thursday

Sunday
Sunday

yesterday
........
yesterday

today
........
today

tomorrow
........
tomorrow

morning
........
morning

noon
........
noon

evening
........
evening

workdays
........
business days

weekend
........
weekend

rain
rain

rainbow
rainbow

wind
wind

snow
snow

spring
spring

summer
summer

fall
autumn

winter
winter

weather forecast

weather forecast

thermometer

thermometer

sunshine

sunshine

cloud

cloud

fog

fog

humidity

humidity

lightning

lightning

thunder

thunder

storm

storm

hail

hail

monsoon

monsoon

flood

flood

ice

ice

January

January

February

February

March

March

April

April

May

May

June

June

July

July

August

August

September
.........................
September

October
.........................
October

November
.........................
November

December
.........................
December

## shapes
## shapes

circle
.........................
circle

square
.........................
square

rectangle
.........................
rectangle

triangle
.........................
triangle

sphere
.........................
sphere

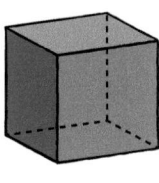

cube
.........................
cube

# colors

## colours

white
white

yellow
yellow

orange
orange

pink
pink

red
red

purple
purple

blue
blue

green
green

brown
brown

gray
grey

black
black

a lot / a little

a lot / a little

angry / calm

angry / calm

beautiful / ugly

beautiful / ugly

beginning / end

beginning / end

big / small

big / small

bright / dark

bright / dark

brother / sister

brother / sister

clean / dirty

clean / dirty

complete / incomplete

complete / incomplete

day / night

day / night

dead / alive

dead / alive

wide / narrow

wide / narrow

edible / inedible

edible / inedible

evil / kind

evil / nice

excited / bored

excited / bored

fat / thin

fat / thin

first / last

first / last

friend / enemy

friend / enemy

full / empty

full / empty

hard / soft

hard / soft

heavy / light

heavy / light

hunger / thirst

hunger / thirst

ill / healthy

sick / healthy

illegal / legal

illegal / legal

intelligent / stupid

intelligent / stupid

left / right

left / right

near / far

near / far

new / used

new / used

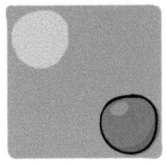

nothing / something

nothing / something

old / young

old / young

on / off

on / off

open / closed

open / closed

quiet / loud

quiet / loud

rich / poor

rich / poor

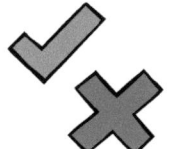

right / wrong

right / wrong

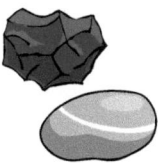

rough / smooth

rough / smooth

sad / happy

sad / happy

short / long

short / long

slow / fast

slow / fast

wet / dry

wet / dry

warm / cool

warm / cool

war / peace

war / peace

**0**

zero

zero

**1**

one

one

**2**

two

two

**3**

three

three

**4**

four

four

**5**

five

five

**6**

six

six

**7**

seven

seven

**8**

eight

eight

**9**

nine

nine

**10**

ten

ten

**11**

eleven

eleven

**12**

twelve

twelve

**13**

thirteen

thirteen

**14**

fourteen

fourteen

**15**

fifteen

fifteen

**16**

sixteen

sixteen

**17**

seventeen

seventeen

**18**

eighteen

eighteen

**19**

nineteen

nineteen

**20**

twenty

twenty

**100**

hundred

hundred

**1.000**

thousand

thousand

**1.000.000**

million

million

English
.................
English

American English
.................
American English

Chinese Mandarin
.................
Mandarin Chinese

Hindi
.................
Hindi

Spanish
.................
Spanish

French
.................
French

Arabic
.................
Arabic

Russian
.................
Russian

Portuguese
.................
Portuguese

Bengali
.................
Bengali

German
.................
German

Japanese
.................
Japanese

I

I

you

you

he / she / it

he / she / it

we

we

you

you

they

they

who?

who?

what?

what?

how?

how?

where?

where?

when?

when?

name

name

behind

behind

in

in

in front of

in front of

over

over

on

on

under

under

beside

beside

between

between

place

place